# The Whimsical World of Boyds Bears

### 25 YEARS AND COUNTIN'!

# The Whimsical World of Boyds® Bears

## 25 YEARS AND COUNTIN'!

### The Silver Anniversary Album

Text by Susan K. Elliott

Reverie

PUBLISHING COMPANY

First Edition/First Printing

To purchase additional copies of this book, please contact:
Reverie Publishing, 130 Wineow Street, Cumberland, MD 21502
888-721-4999

Library of Congress Control Number 2004090403

Project Editor: Krystyna Poray Goddu
Design: Anna Christian
Photography: Courtesy of The Boyds Collection, Ltd.

Printed and bound in Korea

This book is dedicated to . . .

People who enjoy life to the fullest everyday!
The Young and the Young at Heart!
Those Who aren't afraid to Whistle while they Work!
People who aren't afraid to stand up in a crowd and say,
"I'm a Bear Lover and Proud of it!"
Those who believe that Dessert should be part of every meal!
Those who believe that dessert is a Meal!
People who still wear Plaid with Stripes!
People who have beds for their cats and dogs!
The Husbands who pretend the bears in the house are for the kids!
Those who like Fuzzy Stuff!
Those who still believe in Santa Clause . . . we all do!
People who still get excited to see the fireworks on the 4th!
People who think that Chocolate is a food group!
People who aren't afraid to talk to themselves out loud!
All those people who consider shopping a Sport!
People who believe in mid morning and late afternoon naps!
. . . and especially to

All the wonderful Retailers for supportin' us
and bearin' with us through the years!
All of the wonderful collectors for inspiring us . . . for challenging us . . .
and for putting a smile on our face everyday!

Oh yea . . . and to our Moms, Dads, Brothers, Sisters, Uncles, Aunts,
Nieces, Nephews, Cousins, Second Cousins, Grandparents, Great
Grandparents, Neighbors, the Neighbors pets (for not peeing on our lawn),
the Paper Boy (or Girl, sorry), well . . . you get the idea!

**Thanks a Bunch from the Folks at Boyds!!!**

# Contents

# Part 1: The O-Fishull Story

"Do not go where the path may lead; go instead where there is no path and leave a trail."
—EMERSON

# How It All Began

(As Best We Can Remember)

oyds is famous for its friendly, whimsical, folksy at-titude (or at least that's what they tell us), which has its roots in the zany personality and often out-rageous antics of the Head Bean Hisself, aka Gary M. Lowenthal, aka Uncle Bean, founder of the com-pany in 1979. How did such a slightly off-center company come into being? Pure luck? A fluke? Nope . . . believe it or not, it was a lot of hard work, more right decisions than wrong, and many, many won-derful people. Let's start at the very beginning—way back in the years before there was such a thing as Boyds or even the Head Bean—to attempt to answer that question.

## Bringin' Up Bean

Gary Lowenthal traces his roots to a small 1,000-year-old German village called Aschaffenburg, just a hop, skip and an-other hop from Frankfurt. Gary's father, Siegfried, came to the United States at the age of eighteen and worked for his Uncle Gus (a lively character who would later in-spire a bunch of Boyds Stuff). Siegfried even-tually opened his own butcher shop in New York City, and he and his wife, Bea, raised their sons, Steve and Gary, in upper Manhattan. Gary spent many of his younger days in the butcher

shop near the George Washington Bridge, assisting his father and learning the tricks of the trade. He attended P.S. 187 in Manhattan—the inspiration, years later, for a group of animal figurines known as Noah's Pageant Series, B. S. (Bear School, of course!) #187— and then the much-respected and selective Stuyvesant High School, which admitted only the brightest stu-dents. Despite their stan-dards, the Lil' Bean was admitted. Must have been his boyish good looks and hard-to-resist charm.

After graduating from high school in 1965, at the tender age of sixteen, Gary

*Above and below left:* **Mementos from The Head Bean's early life prove his claims that he was a Boy Scout and did indeed graduate from the much-respected, selective Stuyvesant High School in New York City.**

attended Alfred University in upstate New York, where he earned a master's degree in biology, which, according to Gary, he applied later to his business approach. (Sorry Folks, you'll have to wait until he publishes his own book to discover the Lowenthal secrets of building a business. Hey, did you really expect to find the Head Bean's Secrets to Building a Business in this book? Seriously?) He studied hard, as he had in high school, but still found time to enjoy music (and girls!) and make many new friends. This city boy had no idea at the time that he would meet up and lock hearts with a country girl, Justina (better

known as Tina), who grew up in Gettysburg, Pennsylvania. Tina earned a B.S. degree in design and merchandising from Drexel University and went on to a job at Bloomingdale's in Bethesda, Maryland, where she'd meet her future husband.

In the early 1970s, Gary was accepted into the Peace Corps and sent to teach in Lautoka, the second-largest city in Fiji. Asked in later years what he learned in the Peace Corps, Gary said, "That America and New York are not the center of the universe. That material things are not necessary to find happiness. Being in the Peace Corps helped me to become independent and solve my own problems."

When his Peace Corps assignment concluded, Gary took some time out to travel, work and "catch my breath," as he wrote to his parents in a letter sent from New Zealand in 1973. He ended up in New

York and, while bartending a party, met somebody from the well-known Bloomingdale's department store who advised him to enter the store's training program. Once hired, Gary worked his way up to the prestigious position of collection sportswear buyer for Bloomingdale's, which sent him on business trips to Europe, Asia and South America. His many buying trips to Asia taught Gary how to build relationships in China, which would prove fruitful in later years as he developed products for his own company. Gary continued to move up in the ranks at Bloomingdale's, but found he was enjoying the corporate side of his work less and less. He began to fantasize about owning an antiques store in a small town. After being transferred to Rockville, Maryland, he met another Bloomingdale's employee, Tina Unger, soon to become his significant other. It was Tina who encouraged him to quit his job and pursue his dream. (Way to go, Tina!)

*Above:* **Yep, it's The Head Bean disguised as a Bloomingdale's corporate-type.** *Below left:* **Tina poses in front of the antiques store.**

## We're in Bizzniss!

Gary happily jumped down from his ascending star at Bloomingdale's for what he hoped would be a more satisfying, less corporate life, one more in keeping with the ideals of simplicity that he had pursued in the Peace Corps. In 1979, Gary took a leave of absence (in other words . . . see ya . . . it's been fun . . . don't call me, I'll call you) from Bloomingdale's and moved with Tina to the quaint and historic town of Boyds, Maryland, near Washington, D.C. (Are ya payin' attention? Now you know how the company really got its name. The rumors about the company being named after one of Gary's former poker buddies, Boyds McSchister, over a lost bet are not true—otherwise, we'd be known as The McSchister Collection Ltd.)

They found a nineteenth-century Victorian house in the

"More is to be got from one teacher than from two books."
—PROVERB

center of town for their antiques store, The Boyds Collection. They offered quilts, floral arrangements, straw hats decorated by Tina, antiques—practically anything that they could think of was acceptable. Had to pay the electric bill!

After visiting a wildfowl festival on Maryland's eastern shore later in 1979, Gary and Tina were inspired to create decorative duck decoys. They would purchase solid wood blanks, which they would paint, distress (including a gun shot or two!), antique and wax, all by hand. Sales of the decoys boomed. (Tip from yer Ol' Uncle Bean: Don't stand too close when firing a shotgun at your duck decoys to give 'em that ol' worn and weathered look. It's hard to sell headless duck decoys!)

"When you enjoy what you do, every day is a holiday."
—SANTA CLAUS

In these early struggling years, some days went by with no sales at all. Tina remembers coming home once to hear Gary announce a good selling day. "I have good news and bad news," he said. "The good news is that I sold a piece of furniture. The bad news is that it was your bureau." When Tina went upstairs she found all of her clothes sitting in stacks on the floor and her antique bureau gone.

Gary and Tina's devotion to Boyds continued even when they decided to make things 0-fishull and lock hearts for

life. Married on a Thursday, they spent their honeymoon unpacking a twenty-foot truck of merchandise in their store the next day. (Watch out girls ... this guy's a real romantic!)

Their entry into the teddy bear business was as serendipitous as Gary's duck discovery. "In 1982, I saw some Merino wool bears and was fascinated," he says. "Unfortunately, the supplier was always out of stock. So I wrote to the manufacturer in China and had shipments of these bears sent to me." He changed the paw pads to velvet and saw flourishing sales. (Hmmm ... the Head Bean must

have thought!) The Lowenthals were pretty quick to recognize an opportunity. Well, as they say (whoever they is), the rest is history. The bear business was born and the future of the company was about to take a new road.

The Head Bean was gettin' pretty confident about his design abilities, and took

a turn at sculpting. European-style collectible cottages were immensely popular during the mid-1980s. So when asked if he could design a line of resin American-style cottages, the Head Bean said "absolutely, no problem, we can do that ... why, I've been sculpting my entire life ... even helped with that Mt. Rushmore thing in South Dakota ... OK, sure, I'll give it a shot ... what the heck."

A trip to the dental wax store and the itty-bitty tool shop were next on the master sculptor's list. Before you could say Michelangelo (okay, well, it took just

a little longer than that), The Gnomes Homes™ were born, a series of resin cast cottages sculpted and handpainted by Gary. Soon, Gary decided to leave the sculpting to the more experienced, skilled sculptors in China, and focus on the ideas.

With business booming, the company eventually outgrew its Victorian storefront in Boyds, Maryland. They turned for help to the highest of authorities, Reverend Merritt Ednie, the minister who had officiated at their wedding, and took him up on an offer to use the nearby

*Opposite page (bottom left):* **Tina's decorated hats, sold in the antiques store, were among the first Boyds Collection offerings; decorative duck decoys were the couple's next venture.** *Top left:* **The teddy bear business was born with Matthew, made from Australian Merino wool and named after the Lowenthal's son.** *Right:* **In the mid-1980s, Gary began making Gnomes Homes, resin collectible cottages.**

Boyds Presbyterian Church Sunday School building as their warehouse. But before long, they outgrew that space as well, so in 1987 the Lowenthals relocated their home to Gettysburg, Pennsylvania, and moved the warehouse and office to Littlestown, ten miles east of Gettysburg.

> "A dream is the bearer of a new possibility, the enlarged horizon, the great hope."
> —HOWARD THURMAN

## Bears & Hares You Can Trust

The company's move to Pennsylvania in 1987 coincided with a decision to stop producing duck decoys and dive headfirst into the growing world of teddy bears and friends. The same year, the Lowenthals' daughter Bailey was born, inspiring Boyds' soon-to-become-most-popular plush collection!

Over the next few years, key people joined the company, many of them still there more than a decade and a half later. Their stories intertwine with those of the little characters they helped create, known as " . . . Bears & Hares You Can Trust™ . . ." One of the first of these new additions was Jean Grubesky, employee number five. "I basically helped with doing everything. Sometimes we'd sit out on the porch and eat lunch and talk about business plans," says Jean, who contributed to Boyds' growth for sixteen years before retiring in 2003. She remembers a New York gift show in 1990 when Gary said to her, "We can just call this a mom-and-pop, or go for it. What do you think?" And I said, 'Bring it on!'"

In 1987, Boyds began producing bean-bag bears, rabbits, cats and dogs. Gary's design process entailed sketching his

*Above:* **Made from 100 percent Australian Merino Wool fleece, Teddy Hare was part of Boyds' first collection of plush.** *Below:* **In the late 1980s, Boyds focused on creating bears and hares.**

concept and then working directly with the master seamstress to create an initial prototype. He often revised a design twenty or thirty times (those poor seamstresses!) before arriving at the precise "look, feel and personality" he had in mind. In 1988, Boyds presented its first series of bean-filled plush cuties: The J.B. Bean Collection. And in case you've ever wondered, Gary's infamous Head Bean title emerged in 1989 when he was introducing characters in the J.B. Bean Collection to the single Boyds salesperson at the time, Pat Gonder. Gary rattled off: "Rufus R. Bean, Dufus B. Bean, Darryl B. Bean and Dinky B. Bean." He jokingly added, "And I guess that makes me The Head Bean," creating a title that stuck.

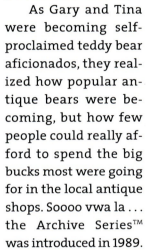

*Above:* **Boyds moved to Littlestown, Pennsylvania, in 1987.** *Below (from left):* **Grandma Bearbug is part of TJ's Best Dressed Collection; Vance Bearsworth is part of the Archive Series.**

Tina quickly caught the bear designing fever, as well. That same year, 1988, she created TJ's Best Dressed Collection of animals with their own wardrobes. The bears were dressed locally, sometimes with just a wisp of lace around the neck— a far cry from the elaborate costumes many Boyds bears wear nowadays. Tina gathered together satin ribbons, bows, nosegays, hand-crocheted lace, and other knickknacks

and, with her husband, sat at the kitchen table and dressed a group of bears. So why TJ? The T is easy—that's Tina—and J stands for her middle name, Jean. Later, she set up a cottage industry to make ever-more intricate costumes, such as felt hats and homespun rompers for each animal.

As Gary and Tina were becoming self-proclaimed teddy bear aficionados, they realized how popular antique bears were becoming, but how few people could really afford to spend the big bucks most were going for in the local antique shops. Soooo vwa la . . . the Archive Series™ was introduced in 1989.

"Many hands make light work."
—PROVERB

These bears were made with the same attention to detail as the old favorites: hockey-stick-style arms, stiffer stuffing, fully jointed with hand-stitched noses—but with one exception. These guys were cheap—we mean, more affordably priced!

Another significant employee joined the company in 1990, after Gary met Liz Smith. Now head of product development (aka VP of Stuff), "Liz is wacky, the heart and soul of the Boyds brand," says Boyds CEO Jan Murley. Gary must have sensed a kindred spirit in Liz. Rather than looking for experience on paper, he wanted people with the right mindset. "One of the biggest things I brought to the company was the ability to think like Gary," says

Liz. "I had the same eye, which is a scary thing!" In 1991, when she was offered the title of Vice President, she said, "I don't want to be Vice President. I want to be Empress of Imports!" Now of course she is known to all as VP of Stuff.

Although she downplays her art background, Liz had always had an artistic side, which she could shift into when needed. Her previous efforts at making fine-art sketches of children and cartoons emerged as a useful skill when she began creating humorous cartoons to fill the empty spaces in early Boyds newsletters. These friendly, newspaper-style publications, first published in 1991 for their retailers and entitled The Boyd's Bear Retail Inquirer, promised " . . . only the BEAR FACTS, . . . all the News that Fits . . . WE PRINT."

A little later that year, the newsletter began a tradition of telling retailers how they could help Boyds win awards. "It was a lot of hard work to bribe all those—that is to say—to have our bears nominated & win these coveted awards. We are winners of the Golden Teddy Award & TOBY Awards. Tell your customers, make a sign, use our sign, use a blackboard in your store, get the magazine, put it in a Lucite frame and put it next to the bear!" Retailers and their customers began to take notice of the fun and quirky views that this small Pennsylvania company was presenting along with its clever and loveable bears.

## We'll Make You Laugh and Sigh

Along the way, the company's guiding slogan emerged: "It has to make you laugh or

*Above:* **Liz Smith's whimsical artwork was a hallmark of the early Boyds newsletters.** *Below:* **An early bean-filled bear, Rufus B. Bean could take on 101 different poses!** *Opposite page (below right):* **Smith Witter II was equally talented.**

make you sigh. If it doesn't do either, we don't want it." This was joined by Boyds' trademarked description, "Folksy with Attitude[SM]," used for its collectibles and plush lines. Part of the humor or emotional draw of Boyds products lies in their names. Company lore holds that in order to come up with better names than the "insulting, demeaning and at the very best, ordinary" ones given to most bears, the entire staff went next door to a local bar (ah . . . we mean local family diner) for inspiration. Soon people began sharing the names of their grandparents and great-grandparents, uncles and aunts, resulting in names such as "Zenis Q. Grimilkin" and "Ophelia R.

"*Individual commitment to a group effort— that is what makes a team work.*"
—VINCE LOMBARDI

Hare." Unusual names continue to be a Boyds hallmark, with examples such as "Indulgenia Q. Bluit . . . Angel of Denial," "Blanche de Bearvoire," "Tallulah Baahead," and "Murgatroyd Von Hindenmoose II" emerging in later years.

Bailey Bear, an 8-inch golden teddy named after Gary and Tina's daughter Bailey Anne Lowenthal, debuted in the fall of 1992. After that year this fashionably dressed teddy appeared each spring and fall in a new outfit; each design was produced for only one year and then retired. Her best friend Emily Babbit the Rabbit appeared in the spring of 1993 and was soon followed by boyfriend Edmund in the fall of 1993. Brother Matthew, inspired by the Lowenthals' son, Matthew Harrison, was introduced in the fall of 1996. (Indy the pooch arrived in the fall of 1997 and was retired before the fall 2002 season.)

**Bailey Bear wearing "Let it Snow" was introduced in 1993.**

Another popular 1992 introduction was The Bubba Bears™, which featured necks and faces that were jointed to look around corners, look up, over and around. Why the name Bubba? Have you ever gone into a diner in a small town? There's always some big old "bear" of a guy (a "Bubba") who almost falls off the stool at the counter, 'cause he's craning his head around so hard to see who's come in. 'Cause nuthin' goes on this town that "Bubba" don't know about. Bubba Bears could do the exact same thing!

Tremendous growth had occurred by the time another long-term staff member,

Chief Operating Officer Chris Bell, joined Boyds in 1992. Hired to be the bookkeeper/comptroller, she became one of about twenty employees. Chris remembers the early days when staff filled customers' orders by taking a grocery cart around the warehouse with the order clipped onto the front of it. "We would look for the items on the order form and put them in the cart," she says. This low-tech approach would surely have made competitors snicker if they had seen it. (Wonder if those grocery carts were ever returned?)

### Boyds Goes Hollywood . . . Sort of

In the early 1990s, Americans were discovering a new way to shop via the QVC television network based in Philadelphia. From morning till late at night, viewers could shop from the comfort of their homes, seeing and learning about all types of new products and then placing orders by phone—which would arrive in their homes in a matter of days. (Talk about paradise for shoppers!) In the same year that QVC founder Joseph Segel (who also founded The Franklin Mint) retired from the shopping network—1993—Gary Lowenthal arrived for his first TV appearance! (Ya don't think one had anything to do with the other, do ya? Nah . . .)

The Head Bean became a regular on QVC, promoting Boyds products. You never knew what The Head Bean was going to do on the air. (He became known as an equal-opportunity offender). The audience, most of them, fell in love with his tongue-in-cheek personality and his on-air chemistry with co-host Mary Beth Roe. Gary was famous for his crazy antics—and

ALL-DAY HOLIDAY SHOPPING

**Viewers never knew what to expect when The Head Bean appeared on QVC with co-host Mary Beth Roe. He might be dressed as a reindeer, or in full Scottish regalia—including a kilt!**

costumes—including being a reindeer, pumpkin, Scotsman, pilgrim, angel, Santa, turkey, Italian salesman and Parisian artist. (Despite his new-found celebrity status, many petitions were signed, letters written, congressmen called to help re-

move Gary from invading the homes of millions. He must be stopped! Just kidding . . . except the letter part) But the folks at QVC are pretty smart. They recognized the chemistry between Gary and Mary Beth was like Ginger Rogers and Fred Astaire, Ozzie and Harriet, Fred and Wilma—well, you get the idea.

After bachillions of laughs, a few tears and a bucket full of apology letters . . . the Head Bean decided to retire from QVC on December 2, 2000, to spend more time with the family. Not to worry, Folks! Boyds very own V.P. of Stuff was pushed on to the stage . . . ooops . . . graciously volunteered to continue the Boyds tradition of entertaining people across the land with the latest creations from Boyds.

But back to 1993—the Head Bean becoming a TV star wasn't the only notable thing that happened that year (just don't tell him we said that). That year also saw a tremendously important introduction that brought unprecedented growth to the company: the Bearstone Collection™ of resin figurines. Based on Boyds' antique-style plush teddy bears, these pieces grabbed attention for their combination of extraordinary detail with a very affordable price. Many of the first-edition figurines (those labeled 1E on the bottom) shot up in value—some almost 5,000 percent within a few years.

The Bearstones immediately drew recognition both from collectors and from the giftware industry. Beginning in 1994, not a year has gone by without at least one award (those bribes did pay off after all!), be it a TOBY, a Golden Teddy or an Award of Excellence, being bestowed on the collection. The Bearstones have been lauded as the most award-winning figurine in the giftware industry.

Gary presented the first three samples of the landmark Bearstone collection at one of his first store appearances, on March 26, 1994, at Koony's Barn, a country gift store in Littlestown, Pennsylvania. "Gary lights up a room," says Liz Smith. "The energy level goes up in a room when he arrives. He is amazingly entertaining." Gary soon incorporated signings into his busy schedule and toured the country to meet collectors; showcase new product concepts; gather feedback; and always ask the customers, "What can we do better?!"

The power of this personal approach combined with the successful QVC shows and the tremendous popularity of the Bearstones became abundantly evident during the 1994 Christmas season. To meet the almost-overwhelming demand for

*Above:* **The Bearstones were an immediate hit when introduced in 1993. Among the earliest were, from left: Father Chrisbear and Son, Bailey Bear with Suitcase and Wilson with Love Sonnets.** *Below:* **Fans always got a big kick out of meeting Gary when he appeared at stores like Koony's Barn.**

"We do not stop playing because we grow old; we grow old because we stop playing."
—ANONYMOUS

their products, the entire Boyds staff left their regular jobs to go into the warehouse to ship orders. A recording on the company answering machine announced, "We're all in the warehouse. We'll get back to you if you have an important question, but just know that if we do call you back, it may be YOUR order that doesn't get filled." Customers were so eager to get their orders in time for Christmas that only two people left messages, and one of those

" . . . at long last, it's finally here . . . a Collector's Club." The club, officially launched in June 1996, was known as the F.o.B Club, The Loyal Order of Friends of Boyds, and described as "A tiny, almost miniscule, slightly off-center collectors society for F.o.B's (Friends of Boyds), who still believe

*Above:* **After The Head Bean retired from his QVC appearances in December 2000, Boyds VP of Stuff, Liz Smith, took over the role, donning bear ears to echo his spirit.** *Left:* **Boyds introduced Father Chrisbear, one of its first dressed Santa Claus Bears in 1991.**

finished by saying, "Oh, I don't know why I left this message. Never mind!"

From that point forward, The Boyds Collection Ltd. grew by leaps and bounds, or, as The Head Bean often said, "Like a mom-and-pop store on steroids!"

## Secret Meeting in Chicago Hotel . . . something shady happening at Boyds!

The fall 1996 edition of The Boyds Bear Gazette announced: "The F.o.B's Are Coming!" The opening story confirmed that

in Bears and Hares you can trust!"

Avid collectors Harry and Millie Croft, then editors of the Bear Tails and Trails newsletter, who had been collecting Boyds pieces since 1993, became the club's first members. Harry Croft remembers the beginning. "When the F.o.B.

Club started (at the International Collectors Expo in Rosemont, Illinois) it was a secret at the convention. Jean Grubesky and Lisa Dickensheets (the first F.o.B club coordinator) made the announcement while Gary was signing that anyone who wanted to join could. A substantial number joined at that point. I kept trying to join and give them my money, but they kept saying, 'later, later.'

"A group of collectors got together that night in the hotel room of Mary Jo Truax (author of three books on Boyds plush). This was the first of the chats with Gary that came later. There were sixty people there. Gary gave me F.o.B. membership Number One. I was so overwhelmed I just couldn't speak. I had tears in my eyes," recalls Harry.

## Bears Ears Appropriate for Any Occasion!

Behind the scenes, a momentous change occurred in April 1998 when The Head Bean sold control of Boyds to an investment group, Kohlberg Kravis Roberts & Co. (KKR). This private investment firm created a partnership with company chairman and founder Gary Lowenthal and its management team. Gary remained the second largest shareholder, but began laying plans to step away from day-to-day management of Boyds. Big changes were ahead, but for Boyds fans, the transition appeared to be a smooth one.

Less than a year later, on Friday, March 5, 1999, more Head Bean History was made when The Boyds Collection Ltd.—the teeny-weeny antique shop/gift company started by Gary and Tina on their kitchen table—began trading on the New York Stock Exchange under the symbol of FOB (Friends of Boyds). High elation met the March 5th offering of Boyds' stock to the public. In a moment that surely epitomizes the dream of every immigrant to America (remember Siegfried?), the Boyds' team was in New York for the first day of public stock trading for Boyds.

"Getting there isn't half the fun, it is the fun."
—ANONYMOUS

*From left:* **The veddy rare red Cavendish was part of the 1994 Christmas critters collection. Well-dressed Eugenia was in T.J.'s Best Dressed collection that year; Fitzgerald D. Bearington.**

On March 5, 1999, Head Bean History was made when the company began trading on the New York Stock Exchange. The Boyds team stood under their flag as public stock trading began under the symbol of FOB.

"It is easier to go down a hill than up, but the view is from the top."
—ARNOLD BENNETT

"My only regret," wrote The Head Bean in the April 1999 issue of The F.o.B. Retail Inquirer, "is that Siggy & Bea, my Mom & Dad, aren't around to see it. Dad was a great 'Stock Picker' & read the Market Reports every evening after a full (and I mean full) day in the Butcher Shop . . . I think it would tickle the ol' boy to know that an Immigrant's Son made it at least part way up the ladder. I think he'd be proud . . . Mom . . . heck, she was proud if I combed my hair once a week."

"The day Gary took the company public was the happiest day of his life," says Liz. "He wore bear ears at the New York Stock Exchange, and I saw him look up and say, 'Yes, Dad, it is the Big Board'."

In August 1999, Boyds announced expansion to Europe with its first overseas sales subsidiary, The Boyds Collection, Ltd., UK, to manage the sale and distribution of Boyds' stuff in the United Kingdom. And just a few months after that, Boyds entered the cyber world with its own website, www.boydsstuff.com. Club members had their very own area where they could find a Boyds Boards for chatting . . . and chat . . . and chat . . . and chat! Seems Boyds fans just love to get together and talk about anything

from politics and religion to debating more serious issues like . . . does the Head Bean wear boxers or briefs? Sorry, Folks . . . some things are still sacred.

## Boyds Convention Attracts Most People Since 1863!

With more than 100,000 club members clamoring for a club event, the folks at Boyds decided it was high time to have the first official Boyds club convention— "a sort of Woodstock for Boyds lovers," says vice-president of marketing Dave Miller. The little town of Gettysburg, however, could only accommodate a maximum of 2,000 people, so a lottery had to be held to select the lucky F.o.B's. When those 2,000 Boyds fanatics invaded the little town of Gettysburg in June 2001 to attend "our veddy own Family Reunion," it was history in the making. Held at Gettysburg College from June 10–13, the F.o.B.'s-only event featured seminars, workshops, live entertainment and a grand finale complete with fireworks.

**The first O-Fishull Family Reunion at Gettysburg College in 2001, attended by 2,000 Friends of Boyds, concluded with a grand fireworks display, below left.**

On the first evening of the convention, Boyds presented an auction of priceless Boyds Stuff. A total of $36,415 was raised for the Starlight Children's Foundation and F.o.B.s had a ton of fun as bids flew fast and furiously.

"The Family Reunion was great," says Dave Reinhart, current editor of Bears Tails and Trails. "They had so many activities going that you couldn't possibly go to all of them . . . you could paint resin or dress a bear. It was awesome."

★ 25 ★

"You never saw anybody who wasn't smiling that weekend," recalls collector Jean Ann Sovereign of Neosho, Missouri. Her husband, Mark, comments: "Anytime we get together with Boyds people we know that these are our friends. And it starts with the Boyds family: Liz is fantastic and it goes all the way down the staff."

## The World's Most HUMONGOUS Teddy Bear Store

One of the company's biggest ventures of the new century has been the building of its own flagship store and museum, Boyds Bear Country™. "Our first Family Reunion gave us the strong message that Boyds is much bigger than bears on shelves," explains COO Chris Bell. "We realized that we needed to build on the feeling of the Family Reunion and to create a mecca for Boyds lovers."

Understanding that their bears are world-famous for their whimsical, laid-back country style, the folks at Boyds spent a long time pondering what kind of structure would best embody that unique Boyds atmosphere. "A slick marble or glass high-rise just wouldn't do," Chris continues. It finally came to them: what better place than a big ol' barn to create that "down on the farm" aura and make people feel right at home.

*Above:* **Groundbreaking for Boyds Bear Country began in spring 2002. It opened that September, enchanting visitors with magical displays of plush creatures, below.**

Set in a former cornfield outside Gettysburg, the five-story, Pennsylvania-style barn structure started taking shape in early spring of 2002. (For a detailed visit, see page 28.) Prior to BBC's September 2002 opening, Chris Bell described its progress. "Boyds Bear Country is—to say the least—a one-of-a-kind family entertainment and shopping destination," she said then. "We don't do anything on a small scale at Boyds, so you can only dream what a spectacular world Boyds Bear Country will be. We can't wait to show off our bears in their very own imaginative environments." Boyds Bear Country opened on September 27th of that year, immediately becoming the area's most popular tourist destination for families.

*Above:* **Liz Smith talks Christmas bears with the** *Today* **show's Matt Lauer.** *Left:* **The Nursery is a favorite stop for families at Boyds Bear Country.**

## Wow . . . that 25 years went by fast!

How does one reconcile Boyds today with the little mom-and-pop company started in 1979 on a kitchen table? Unlike the summer of 2003 blackout that started with one power failure before rippling through the entire Northeast grid system, Boyds' growth represents a series of creative power surges. One good idea leads to another, giving Boyds fans even more to appreciate, and to anticipate.

Liz Smith, often called "the Keeper of the Gate" at the company, remembers, "Originally we created twenty-five new bears a season, then thirty to thirty-five, then we asked, 'Is forty-five too much?' Now we introduce new products twice a year—about 300 per season, plus special orders and QVC items.

"Gary challenged people to reach beyond themselves to do their best," she continues. "He brought that out in people. He was tenacious in his creativity."

Chris Bell believes that employees' loyalty to Boyds goes deeper than just getting the next paycheck. "It changes here all the time," she says. "The staff goes wherever they're needed. Everything is our job. We don't ever say, 'that's not my job'. We're always willing to try new things, to make catalogs better, find a way to ship better.

"When you work at a company that has changed as much as ours and has allowed its employees to be involved in what happens (mostly out of necessity, too much to do, too little time), it makes us feel like a part of the company belongs to us," she emphasizes. "We've developed a sense of responsibility for the company and a lot of pride in its success."

Liz echoes this thought, saying, "Boyds is my secondary family here now. Bear people are the most wonderful people on the face of the earth. There are no mean teddy bear people." She sums up the Boyds' philosophy by saying, "The culture of Boyds is different from most companies because of its tongue-in-cheek humor and its irreverence. I want to keep that alive in the company. It's essential to keep an irreverent view of the world. We say, 'If we're not laughing we're not doing it right.' "

*"Great persons are able to do great kindnesses."*
—CERVANTES

★ 27 ★

# Part 2: Boyds Bear Country

"The balance between work and play should always be tipped toward play."
—ANONYMOUS

Down Home at

the Big Ol' Barn

O nce upon a time, family farms with neatly planted fields made up the landscape around Gettysburg, Pennsylvania. Today many small farms are still there, but at 75 Cunningham Road, the gentle sound of wind blowing through corn stalks has been replaced by a hubbub of activity at Boyds Bear Country—The World's Most Humongous Teddy Bear Store. An enormous mural of a cuddly-looking teddy bear resting on a split-rail fence welcomes visitors, who quickly realize they are about to experience something special.

This is no ordinary teddy bear store. Home to more than 70,000 bears, hares and other critters in a massive five-story red barn, Boyds Bear Country promises that visitors will "meet friends ya never knew you had and walk away with memories to last a lifetime!"

Signs bearing good advice like: "Don't like living in the fast lane? Then don't turn in here!" greet guests, along with The Head Bean Hisself, in the form of a larger-than-life bronze statue. A one-of-a-kind shopping experience, lots of hands-on activities for all ages, a free museum and plenty of good eats bring Boyds lovers back to Boyds Bear Country over and over again. You come, too.

*Opposite page:* **Folks call it the largest bank barn constructed in the Western Hemisphere and yep, Boyds Bear Country was inspired by the design of Pennsylvania bank barns. With 120,000 square feet of shopping space, it sure is The World's Most Humongous Teddy Bear Store.** *Above:* **A fireworks extravaganza tops off July 4th festivities.**

*Above:* **Everything's comin' up daisies at Bailey's Seed Shack.** *Left:* **Bears and friends kick back and enjoy freshly squeezed lemonade in a springtime display.** *Below:* **The Head Bean Hisself (in bronze), waits outside the entrance to say hi.** *Opposite page:* **Pandora, a 40-inch extra-huggable panda is also on hand to greet guests.**

*Opposite page:* **Boyds Bear Country even has runnin' water . . . an indoor creek meanders right through the springtime display. If ya decide to cross the bridge, be sure to take a peek at the bears and friends who live beneath. Never know who yer gonna see!** *Above:* **Fittin' right into the barn-style of Boyds Bear Country, Boyds barnyard friends—chickens, roosters, pigs, country kittens and cows—make a lively barnyard display.** *Left:* **There's tons of fun at Boyds Bear Country for kids . . . of all ages! There's so much to see and do—shoppin', of course, and live entertainment, family activities, special events scheduled all year long, plus plenty of good eats!**

# BOYDS BEAR COUNTRY

*Left:* **Even on the greyest day, you'll find springtime flowers bloomin' and Boyds garden and farm friends haulin' in fresh produce!**
*Above (from top):* **On the second floor, yer all invited to Noah's Ark and a Jungle Adventure. The life-size ark is filled with Boyds' plush critters—from tigers and camels to monkeys, elephants, giraffes and even a moose or two! A human-size Noah welcomes one and all to step a li'l closer and peek inside the portholes. Kids (and grown-ups, too!) love to create their own bears from start to finish at Digby's Super Duper Bear Factory™! The factory experience includes time cards and hard hats and a magical "rainbow bean" filling for the new bears. And of course there's always your supervisors lookin' over yer shoulder!**

*Above:* **Everybody loves the patriotic bears and the stars, stripes, vintage and antique props in the Americana displays! Boyds Bear Country exclusives Mason and Dixon are a hit with history and Civil War buffs. The bears pay tribute to Confederate and Union soldiers in their costumes, which were designed by a nineteenth-century clothing expert.**

*Left:* **A humongous cuddly-looking teddy resting on a split-rail fence waves a welcome to all who approach Boyds Bear Country. The 72-foot-wide by 47-foot-high mural, designed by Boyds artist Amy Routson and painted by muralist Wane Fettro, is your first hint that there's never gonna be a dull moment— you are about to experience something out of the ordinary!**

# Part 3: Boyds in All Seasons

> "Wherever you are, it is your friends who make your world."
> —WILLIAM JONES

# Bears, Hares

& Friends

# SPRING IS IN THE AIR!

"Sweet spring,
full of sweet
days..."
—GEORGE HERBERT

# SPRING IS IN THE AIR!

"A single rose
could be my garden...
a single friend
my world."
—BUSCAGLIA

"Friendship is the only glue that will ever hold the world together."
—WOODROW WILSON

*Opposite page:*
**Verna and Shirlie . . . Recipe for Friendship, 4 1/2 inches**

*From top:*
**Rachael and Phoebe . . . Girls Night Out, 3 1/2 inches; Olive Leafowitz with Forest Friends . . . Joy Ride, 4 1/2 inches**

"He who plants
a garden, plants
happiness."
—CHINESE PROVERB

# SPRING IS IN THE AIR!

"Some things are
stored in the heart
and not in the mind."
—UNKNOWN

*Opposite page
(clockwise from left):*
**Bailey, 8 inches; Emily Babbit,
8 inches; Edmund, 8 inches**

*From top:*
**Coco DeBearvoire, 6 inches;
JoJo DeBearvoire, 6 inches**

# SPRING IS IN THE AIR!

"One single grateful thought raised to heaven is the most perfect prayer."
—G. E. LESSING

*Opposite page*
*(clockwise from top left):*
**Michele S. Hopplebuns, 9 inches;**
**Dazey Ewe, 11 inches; Prissie**
**Hopplebuns, 12 inches; Kimmy,**
**10 inches; Brittney Q. Hopplebuns,**
**8 inches**

*From top:*
**Miracle Gardenglow, 8 inches;**
**Key Lime Thumpster, 10 inches**

Delanie D. Hopplebuns, 16 inches

"You're only here for a short visit. Don't hurry. Don't worry. And be sure to smell the flowers along the way."
—WALTER C. HAGEN

*From top:*
**Rosalie Bloomengrows, 10 inches;**
**Webster Hopplebuns, 8 inches**

*Opposite page:*
**Vanessa V. Fluffypaws, 16 inches**

# SPRING IS IN THE AIR!

🐾

"From small
beginnings come
great things."
—PROVERB

🐾

"Dreaming is to
think by moonlight
by the light of
an inner moon."
—JULES RENARD

*Opposite page
(clockwise from top left):*
**Wubbie, 12 inches; Silly,
12 inches; Kiddie, 12 inches;
Moo Moo, 12 inches**

*From top:*
**Kibby T. Beansley, 14 inches;
Catterina Cuddlepuss, 16 inches**

"We find delight in the beauty and happiness of children that makes the heart too big for the body."
—RALPH WALDO EMERSON

*Opposite page:*
**Momma McNew with Hugsley,
10 inches**

**Grammy with Babykins . . .
Love Never Spoils, 4¼ inches**

*Clockwise from top left:*
**Bailey, 8 inches; Little Bearpeep and Friends, 12 inches; Humpy Dumpy, 10 inches; Huff P. Wolf with Bacon, Porkchop & Hamlette, 10 inches; Huff P. Wolf with Bacon, Porkchop & Hamlet . . . Hard Work Pays Off, 2³/₄ inches; Ol' Mother McBear . . . The More the Merrier, 5 inches; Lil' Miss Muffet . . . What's In the Bowl?, 4¹/₂ inches; Humpy Dumpy . . . All Cracked Up, 4¹/₄ inches; Lil' Bear Peep . . . Got Sheep?, 4 inches; Old Mother Gooseberry . . . Once Upon A Time, 4 inches; Lil' Red with B.B. Woff . . . Going to Grandma's, 5 inches**

"Once upon a time—those spellbinding words transport us into the magical world of fairy tales and nursery rhymes."
—CAROLINE CAMPBELL

"Animals are such agreeable friends—they ask no questions. They pass no criticisms."
—GEORGE ELIOT

**Olde Mother Goose & Co.,
10 inches**

*Opposite page:*
**Mr. Noah and Friends,
14 inches**

"We are here on earth to do good to others."
—W.H. AUDEN

"May your troubles be less and your blessings be more and nothing but happiness come through the door."
—IRISH BLESSING

*Clockwise from top left:*
**Coo & Lou, 1½ inches; Noah, 8 inches; Monkey See & Monkey Do, 3½ inches; Packy & Derma Trunkspace, 3½ inches; Stretch & Skye Longnecker, 3½ inches; Zeiggy & Roary Tigertooth, 3½ inches; Mrs. Noah, 7 inches; Lawrence & Sheherazade O'Sand, 3½ inches; Lucy & Ricky Bandito, 3½ inches; Alice & Joey Outback, 3½ inches; Iggy & Lou Frostbite, 3½ inches; Hsing Hsing & Ling Ling Wongbruin, 3½ inches; Charlotte & Wilbur Hamstein, 3½ inches; Bessie & Chuck Moosley, 3½ inches; Babs and Baab Woolsley, 3½ inches; Dale and Ilona Moosley, 3½ inches**

# SPRING IS IN THE AIR!

"Darling, what is
that? Are you sure
it is a hat?"
—OGDEN NASH

*Opposite page:*
**Margaret with Kristen . . . There
Goes the Budget, 4 inches**

*From top:*
**Adeline LaBearsley, 12 inches;
Claudette Prissypuss, 12 inches**

Mrs. Everlove, 12 inches;
Mr. Everlove, 12 inches

*Opposite page:*
Mr. & Mrs. Everlove . . . From
This Day Forward, 4 inches

CELEBRATIN' SUMMER!

"Liberty and independence forever!"
–DAVY CROCKETT

*Clockwise from left:*
Tyler Glorybear, 8 inches;
Tucker P. Woofensniff, 10 inches;
Liza Glorybear, 16 inches; Jennie
Glorybear, 14 inches; Mamie
Glorybear, 6 inches; Edith Glorybear,
6 inches; Ike Glorybear, 10 inches;
Glory, 6 inches

"Oh never mind the fashion. When one has a style of one's own, it is always twenty times better."
—MARGARET OLIPHANT

*From top:*
**Thaddeus Von Bruin, 16 inches;**
**Patrick Bearsevelt, 6 inches**

*Opposite page:*
**Gloria Bearsevelt, 14 inches**

"I don't have anything against work. I just figure why deprive somebody who really enjoys it?"
—DOBIE GILLIS

BOYDS GAZETTE
GOOD BEARS GONE BAD...

SUMMER HEAT-WAVE Leads to LEMONADE Shortage DETAILS ON PG 3T

**Norman Doinuttin . . .**
**Sorry Girls, He's Taken, 4 inches**

*Opposite page:*
**Bailey, 8 inches; Emily Babbit; 8 inches**

*Patriotic Greetings from 1773*

*Opposite page:*
**Martha, Dolly and George . . .
An American Traditional
Musical, 6³/₄ inches**

*From left:*
**Yankee Doodlebear . . . Stars and
Stripes Forever, 2⁷/₈ inches;
Sammy Bearmerican . . . I Pledge
Allegiance, 4 inches**

GOD BLESS AMERICA

"America is a willingness
of the heart."
—F. SCOTT FITZGERALD

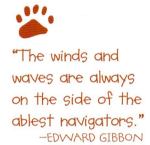

"The winds and waves are always on the side of the ablest navigators."
—EDWARD GIBBON

**Radcliffe Fitzbruin, 16 inches**

*Opposite page
(clockwise from left):*
**Maris Q. Yachtley, 16 inches;
Skip B. Yachtley, 6 inches;
Morgan T. Yachtley with Bill,
14 inches; Rowen Yachtley,
10 inches;  Webb Q. Yachtley,
8 inches; Marina Yachtley,
10 inches**

"I have a simple
philosophy.
Fill what's empty.
Empty what's full."
—ALICE ROOSEVELT LONGWORTH

# CELEBRATIN' SUMMER!

"There are two days in the week on which I never worry: one is yesterday and the other is tomorrow."
—P.J. BURDETTE

*Opposite page:*
**Woodrow T. Bearington, 12 inches**

*From top:*
**Cousin Marty with Rover, 9 inches;**
**Layana Rugsley, 40 inches**

"What is important
is that one is
capable of love.
It is perhaps
the only glimpse
we are permitted
of eternity."
–HELEN HAYES

*From top:*
**Dale & Ilona . . . Under the
Mooseltoe, 3 inches; Sissie and
Squirt . . . Big Helper, Lil' Sipper,
4 1/4 inches**

*Opposite page:*
**Harry & Millie . . . Through the
Years, 4 inches**

"BEST FRIENDS WEATHER ANY STORM"

"How doth the little busy bee improve each shining hour and gather honey all the day from every opening flower!"
—ISAAC WATTS

GARDEN THYME

*Clockwise from top left:*
**Jeb MacDonald, 12 inches;
Emerson T. Penworthy, 9 inches;
Rosie O'Pigg, 11 inches; Willie B.
Bacon, 16 inches; Porker P. Piggytoes,
8 inches; Abbie Mae Woolsey,
11 inches; Archie Strutencrow,
9 inches; Clancy G. Hydrant, Jr.,
10 inches; Clovis Moosdale, 8 inches;
Shiloh P. Poochdale, 10 inches;
Romano B. Grated, 6 inches; Munster
Q. Fondue, 6 inches; Corabelle
Hoofenutter, 11 inches**

"A good farmer is
a handy man with
a sense of Humus."
—E.B. WHITE

"Good company
in a journey makes
the way to seem
the shorter"
—ISAAK WALTON

*From top:*
**Merle B. Squirrel, 7 inches;**
**Bucky Beaverdam, 10 inches;**
**Flash, 9 inches**

*Opposite page*
*(clockwise from left):*
**Ripple, 4 inches; Orvis T. Fisher**
**with Tad, 12 inches; Nettie**
**Fisher, 10 inches; Shawnee**
**Fisher, 16 inches; Lily the Frog**
**Tug Along, 3 inches; Bobber,**
**6 inches**

"Time is but
the stream I go
a-fishing in."
—HENRY DAVID THOREAU

"Sometimes I sits and thinks and sometimes I just sits."
—SATCHEL PAIGE

FOR THE BIRDS

"Life is fragile.
Handle with prayer."
—ANONYMOUS

Opposite page:
**Hector Hugsley, 30 inches**

Clockwise from top left:
**Robin's For the Birds Birdhouse,
10 inches; Emily Babbit, 8 inches;
Bailey, 8 inches; Tweeters Tug
Along, 2 inches; Edmund,
8 inches**

# CELEBRATIN' SUMMER!

"Life is short, and it's up to you to make it sweet."
—SARAH LOUISE DELANEY

"Nature wants us to enjoy life to the full."
—SAINTE-BEUVE

*Opposite page*
*(clockwise from upper left):*
**Summer Sanditoes, 8 inches;**
**Sandy Sanditoes, 10 inches;**
**Wade N. Sanditoes with Buster**
**the Crab, 8 inches; Shelby T. Sanditoes, 6 inches**

*From top:*
**Kendallyn H. Sugarcone, 16 inches;**
**Purcilla P. Sugarcone, 11 inches**

"Dance is the
hidden language
of the soul."
—MARTHA GRAHAM

From top:
**Bailey... Swing Time, 4 inches;**
**Ashley Pirouette... The Recital,**
**2 1/2 inches**

*Opposite page:*
**Amanda and Michael...**
**String Section, 4 inches**

"After silence that which comes nearest to expressing the inexpressible is music."
—ALDOUS HUXLEY

"Try to make
yourself remarkable
by some talent
or other."
—SENECA

WILL WORK FOR PEANUTS

*Opposite page (from top):*
**Darwin Monkbury, 8 inches;**
**Dalton Monkbury, 8 inches;**
**Hannibel Trunkster, 16 inches**

*From left:*
**Mr. McFarkle, 14 inches;**
**Mr. Bojingles, 14 inches**

*Clockwise from left:*
**Momma McVeggie and the Sweetpeas, 14 inches;
Wabbit McVeggie, 11 inches; April Mae McVeggie,
16 inches; Edgar Eggplant, 5 1/2 inches; Cari
Carrot, 5 1/2 inches; Tommy Tomato, 5 1/2 inches;
April Mae's Veggie Patch Birdhouse, 12 inches;
Radcliff McVeggie, 10 inches; Stew T. Mater . . .
Catch-Up, 2 1/4 inches; E. P. Parmesan . . . Grate
Finish, 2 inches; Jack Q. Rabbit . . . Peelin' Out,
3 inches; Polly Peapod, 5 1/2 inches; You Say
Tomato . . . Tug Along, 3 inches**

"Gardening is a growing experience . . . first it takes over your yard. Then your life."
—P.T. DIGSALOT

VEGGIE PATCH

VEGETABLE PATCH

# HARVESTIN' FALL'S PLEASURES

"Give us the luxuries of life and we will dispense with its necessities."
—JOHN LOTHROP MOTL

Pears
5¢

TEACHERS COUNT !

*From top:*
**Betty B. Learnin, 10 inches;**
**Kendall B. Learnin, 12 inches;**
**Miss Wisely, 6 inches**

*Opposite page (from top):*
**The Boyds Bearly A School,**
**4¹/₂ inches; Amy B. Bearsdale . . .**
**Lunchtime Yet?, 4 inches**

"The future belongs
to those who believe
in their dreams."
—ELEANOR ROOSEVELT

"Books and friends
should be few,
but good."
—PROVERBS

"Rain, rain go away,
come again
another day."
—ANONYMOUS

**Noah, 14 inches; Noah's
Umbrella, 9 1/2 inches**

*Opposite page:*
**Clem Cladiddlebear, 30 inches**

THE WONDERS OF SCIENCE IN MODERN LIFE

THE WONDERS OF SCIENCE IN MODERN LIFE

"Life's too short to come unraveled."
—ANONYMOUS

# HARVESTIN' FALL'S PLEASURES!

"Big shots are only little shots who keep shooting."
—CHRISTOPHER MORLEY

"Winning isn't everything, but wanting to is."
—VINCE LOMBARDI

*Opposite page:*
**T.D. Gridiron . . . Touch Down!,
4 inches**

*From top:*
**Dunkin', 10 inches;
Pat T. Spiker, 10 inches**

"Nothing is so strong
as gentleness,
nothing so gentle
as real strength."
—FRANCIS DE SALES

*Opposite page:*
**Florence Gentlecare . . .
Touching Lives, 3¹/₄ inches**

*From top:*
**Patrick and His Hero . . .
When I Grow Up, 4¹/₄ inches;
Elliot . . . The Hero, 4¹/₂ inches**

# HARVESTIN' FALL'S PLEASURES!

"We can do no great things—only small things with great love."
—MOTHER TERESA

*Opposite page:*
**Chief Buckley with Jennifer . . . To the Rescue, 3¹/₄ inches**

*From top:*
**Florence Nightenbear, 12 inches; Karen Gentletouch with Lil' Bearybutt . . . Kind Heart, 4¹/₂ inches**

"We must always have old memories and young hopes."
—HOUSSAYE

"All human wisdom is summed up in two words—wait and hope."
—DUMAS

*Opposite page:*
**Abbot Q. Beanster, 16 inches**

**Will B. Missingyou, 8 inches**

MISS YOU

# HARVESTIN' FALL'S PLEASURES!

"Freedom is the last, best hope of earth."
—ABRAHAM LINCOLN

"Hope is a waking dream."
—ARISTOTLE

*Opposite page:*
**McBruin . . . To Serve with Honor, 5 1/4 inches**

**Gomer Q. Beanster, 14 inches**

"It is not real work unless you would rather be doing something else."
—J.M. BARRIE

*From top:*
**Holden T. Punkinbeary, 8 inches;**
**Rusty & Scardycrow, 14 inches**

*Opposite page (from top):*
**Einstein Q. ScaredyBear, 10 inches;**
**Polly Quignapple, 10 inches**

"The pursuit of treats is a blessing in disguise."
—E.E. SMITH

*From left:*
**Inkley Boocat, 5¹/₂ inches; Samantha Sneakypuss, 8 inches; Samantha Sneakypuss, 8 inches; Felina B. Catterwall, 8 inches; Sabrina P. Catterwall, 8 inches; Jack O. Lantern, 13 inches; Felina B. Catterwall, 8 inches; Mrs. Partridge, 9 inches**

# HARVESTIN' FALL'S PLEASURES!

*Opposite page
(clockwise from left):*
**T. G. Trickster, 8 inches; Sooty
P. Pussyfoot, 7 inches; Patsie
Punkley, 10 inches; Scardy Cat
Tug Along, 2½ by 4 inches;
Inkley Boocat, 5½ inches;
Paula Punkley, 6 inches**

*From top:*
**Conner D. Devilbear, 10 inches;
Zelda Z. Witchpuss, 11 inches**

"From ghoulies and ghosties
and long-leggedy beasties
and things that go bump in
the night . . ."
—TRADITIONAL SCOTTISH PROVERB

# HARVESTIN' FALL'S PLEASURES!

*Opposite page*
*(clockwise from top left):*
**Aubrey T. Autumnfest, 16 inches;**
**Mahoney S. Mooseltoof, 14 inches;**
**Meg Autumnfest, 10 inches;**
**Punkin B. Beary, 8 inches; Tina**
**Autumnfest, 6 inches; Ervin**
**Autumnfest, 14 inches**

*From top:*
**Redford T. Woodsbeary, 16 inches;**
**B. Autumnfest, 12 inches**

"Clothes make the
man. Naked people
have little or no
influence on society."
—MARK TWAIN

★123★

*From left:*
**Roma Applesmith, 16 inches;**
**Sable B. Bearsdale, 14 inches;**
**First Ever Bean Bear, 10 inches;**
**Jasper McBobble, 10 inches**

BEARS & FRIENDS

CAT
BEAR
DOG

"Knowledge is a treasure but practice is the key to it."
—PROVERB

WELCOME TO OUR WINTER

"Winter dances
with frost and holly
on crystalline,
cold clear nights."
—UNKNOWN

# WONDERLAND!

*Clockwise from left:*
**Carly Crystalfrost, 10 inches; Natasha Crystalfrost, 8 inches; Mariah Crystalfrost, 16 inches; Sarabeth Crystalfrost, 12 inches; Dean S. Bearsalot, 21 inches; I.C. Crystalfrost, 5 inches; Snowy Crystalfrost, 6 inches; Chandler Chrystalfrost, 10 inches**

"Always listen to experts. They'll tell you what can't be done and why. Then go do it."
—ROBERT HEINLEIN

# WELCOME TO OUR WINTER WONDERLAND!

*Opposite page (clockwise from left):*
**Victoria L. Plumbeary, 16 inches;**
**Christine P. Plumbeary, 8 inches;**
**Erin Plumbeary, 6 inches;**
**Christiana LaBearsley, 6 inches**

**Bailey, 8 inches**

"Grace was in all her steps, heav'n in her eyes."
—JOHN MILTON

"Time for a little something."
—A.A. MILNE

*Opposite page:*
**Mr. Mocha Java Mooselbean . . .
Doubleshot, 4¹/₄ inches**

*From left:*
**Morley P. Moosetrax, 14 inches;
Malley Q. Mooselfluff, 10 inches**

"Everyone is kneaded out of the same dough, but not baked in the same oven."
—PROVERB

**Humphrey T. Bigfoot, 18 inches**

*Opposite page (clockwise from left):* **Jilian G. Gingerbeary, 14 inches; Mary Kate Gingerbeary, 8 inches; Kassie Gingerbeary, 10 inches; G.B. Gingerbeary, 6 inches; Gingerbeary Tug Along, 4 inches**

**Boyds Bearly-Built Villages . . . Boydstown** *(from left):* **Madge's Beauty Salon and Bait Shop, 4³/₄ inches; Bearly Well Clinic, 4³/₄ inches; Volunteer Fire Station, 5¹/₄ inches; Cocoa's House of Chocolates, 5¹/₄ inches; Boyds Bearly a School, 4¹/₂ inches; The Chapel in the Woods, 6¹/₂ inches**

"Christmas waves a magic wand over this world . . ."
—NORMAN VINCENT PEALE

"May the Peace of the Season be in your heart."

*Clockwise from left:*
**Annabelle Dickens, 12 inches; Abbott Q. Beanster, 16 inches; Marley Dickens, 14 inches; Vivian Q. Dickens, 16 inches; Isabelle Dickens, 8 inches; Charles the Dog Tug Along, 3 inches; Charles, 6 inches**

"I will honor Christmas in my heart and try to keep it all the year."
—EBENEZER SCROOGE

*Opposite page:*
**Chris Kringlebeary, 14 inches**

*From top:*
**Mr. Kringle, 16 inches;**
**Nickolas S. Hugsley, 30 inches**

★139★

J.W. Van Winkle & Snuggles,
14 inches

Joelle, 5½ inches;
Krystle B. Bearbright,
16 inches

"*It is Christmas in the heart that puts Christmas in the air.*"
—W. T. ELLIS

*Clockwise from left:*
**Lil' C.C., 3¹/₂ inches; H.B. Starcatcher, 5 inches; Polarsox, 5 inches; Frazier, 6 inches; Albert Merrybeary, 8¹/₂ inches; Keifer B. Effington, 10 inches; Klondike, 14 inches; Christmas Candy Tug Along, 1¹/₄ inches; Derby Scruffles, 8 inches; The North Pole Express; Derry O. Berry, 6¹/₂ inches; Rudy Pitoody, 11 inches; Bearstone Little Star of Nativity Pac; Bearstone Followin' Yonder Star Nativity; Lil Ginger, 3¹/₂ inches**

# WELCOME TO OUR WINTER WONDERLAND!

*"It's not the years in your life that count. It's the life in your years."*
—ABRAHAM LINCOLN

*"Dreams do come true, if we only wish hard enough."*
—JAMES BARRIE

*Opposite page:*
**Cindy McSnoozle with Cuddles, 10 inches**

*From left:*
**Dover D. Windsor, 8 inches;
Bristol. B. Windsor, 8 inches**

# WELCOME TO OUR WINTER WONDERLAND!

Opposite page
(clockwise from top left):
**Mrs. Kringlebeary, 14 inches;
C.C. Peekers, 6 inches; Cindy
McSnoozle with Cuddles, 10
inches; Maury McSnoozle with
Maddie, 8 inches; Snackers
McSnoozle, 5 inches; Stuart
McSnoozle, 10 inches**

From top:
**A.J. Blixen, 8 inches;
Winter Mintly, 16 inches**

"A little warmth, a
little light, of love's
bestowing—and so,
good night!"
—GEORGE LOUIS PALMELLA
BUSSON DU MAURIER

"It is a happy talent
to know how to play."
—RALPH WALDO EMERSON

**Pandora, 40 inches**

*Opposite page
(clockwise from left):*
**Mindy P. Elfbeary with Molly,
9 inches; Trevor T. Elfbeary with
Giddyap, 12 inches; Gregory B.
Elfbeary with Gus, 10 inches;
Moxley . . . The Rocking Horse,
16½ inches; Kirby Elfbeary with
Gallop, 8 inches; Moxley Von
Mooseltoes, 8 inches**

"There is majesty
in simplicity."
—ALEXANDER POPE

"We do not
remember days,
we remember
moments."
—CESARE PAVESE

*Opposite page (from left):*
**Bailey, 8 inches; Matthew,
8 inches; Edmund, 8 inches**

*From top:*
**Fargo Grizwold, 16 inches;
Matthew, 8 inches**

*Clockwise from left:*
**Ludwigg V. Burrbruin, 14 inches; Yeti A. Bominable, 18 inches; Franz Farklefrost, 10 inches; Karina Burrbruin, 16 inches; Leisel L. Burrbruin, 8 inches; Fritzle Farklefrost, 8 inches; Franklefrost Tug Along, 3 1/2 inches; Inga B. Burrbruin, 6 inches; Eric Burrbruin, 10 inches, Gustaf Mooseltoff, 12 inches**

"We are shaped and fashioned by what we love."
—JOHANN WOLFGANG VON GOETHE

# WELCOME TO OUR WINTER WONDERLAND!

"*I have never been able to understand why it is that just because I am unintelligible nobody understands me.*"
—MILTON MAYMER

*Opposite page:*
**Marlena Beargeauz & Deitrich, 16 inches**

**First Ever Bean Bear, 10 inches**

*Opposite page (from top):*
**Miss Truelove's Heart's Desire,
3¹/₂ inches; Bailey . . . Heart's
Desire, 3 inches**

**Hugs N. Kisses, 6 inches**

"A family is a little world created by love."
—ANONYMOUS

Gary, Tina, Matt & Bailey . . .
From Our Home to Yours

*Opposite page:*
**Sinclair Bearsford, 16 inches**

♥ THE FAMILY ♥

"Go confidently
in the direction
of your dreams.
Live the life
you've imagined."
—THOREAU

# INDEX TO PART 3

★160★